THE
FURIES

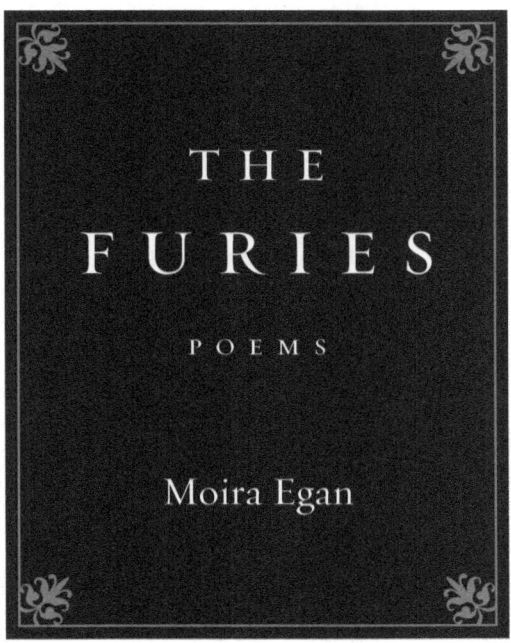

LOUISIANA STATE
UNIVERSITY PRESS
BATON ROUGE

Published by Louisiana State University Press
lsupress.org

Copyright © 2025 by Moira Egan
All rights reserved. Except in the case of brief quotations used in articles or reviews, no part of this publication may be reproduced or transmitted in any format or by any means without written permission of Louisiana State University Press.

LSU Press Paperback Original

DESIGNER: Michelle A. Neustrom
TYPEFACES: Arno Pro, text; Requiem Text, display

COVER IMAGES: Wall frescoes from the Villa della Farnesina at the Palazzo Massimo, National Roman Museum. Photograph of the top fresco by Simona Sansonetti. Courtesy of the Ministry of Culture—National Roman Museum, Photographic Archive.

LIBRARY OF CONGRESS CATALOGING-IN-PUBLICATION DATA

Names: Egan, Moira, 1962– author.
Title: The furies : poems / Moira Egan.
Description: Baton Rouge : Louisiana State University Press, 2025.
Identifiers: LCCN 2025018563 (print) | LCCN 2025018564 (ebook) | ISBN 978-0-8071-8498-1 (cloth) | ISBN 978-0-8071-8577-3 (epub) | ISBN 978-0-8071-8578-0 (pdf)
Subjects: LCGFT: Poetry
Classification: LCC PS3605.G357 F87 2025 (print) | LCC PS3605.G357 (ebook) | DDC 811/.6—dc23/eng/20250611
LC record available at https://lccn.loc.gov/2025018563
LC ebook record available at https://lccn.loc.gov/2025018564

Εὐμενίδων II

θυμίαμα, ἀρώματα.

Κλῦτέ μευ, Εὐμενίδες μεγαλώνυμοι, εὔφρονι βουλῇ,
ἁγναὶ θυγατέρες μεγάλοιο Διὸς χθονίοιο,
Φερσεφόνης τ', ἐρατῆς κούρης καλλιπλοκάμοιο,
αἵ πάντων καθορᾶτε βίον θνητῶν ἀσεβούντων,
τῶν ἀδίκων τιμωροί, ἐφεστηκυῖαι ἀνάγκῃ,
κυανόχρωτοι ἄνασσαι, ἀπαστράπτουσαι ἀπ' ὄσσων
δεινὴν ἀνταυγῇ φάεος σαρκοφθόρον αἴγλην·
ἀΐδιοι, φοβερῶπες, ἀπόστροφοι, αὐτοκράτειραι,
λυσιμελεῖς οἴστρῳ, βλοσυροί, νύχιαι, πολύποτμοι,
νυκτέριαι κοῦραι, ὀφιοπλόκαμοι, φοβερῶπες,
ὑμέας κικλήσκω γνώμαις ὁσίῃσι πελάζειν.

To the Furies

The Fumigation, with Aromatics

Hear me, illustrious Furies, mighty nam'd,
Terrific pow'rs, for prudent counsel fam'd;
Holy and pure, from Jove terrestrial born
And Proserpine, whom lovely locks adorn:
Whose piercing sight, with vision unconfin'd,
Surveys the deeds of all the impious kind:
On Fate attendant, punishing the race
(With wrath severe) of deeds unjust and base.
Dark-colour'd queens, whose glittering eyes are bright
With dreadful, radiant, life-destroying light:
Eternal rulers, terrible and strong,
To whom revenge, and tortures dire belong;
Fatal and horrid to the human sight,
With snaky tresses wand'ring in the night;
Hither approach, and in these rites rejoice,
For ye, I call, with holy, suppliant voice.

—Orphic Hymn no. 70

CONTENTS

I. GROUP THERAPY FOR THE FEMALE CHARACTERS OF *THE ODYSSEY*

Penelope 3
Siren 4
Circe 5
Scylla 6
Charybdis 7
Nausikaa 8
Eurykleia 9

II. SORORAL

Arachne 13
Elegy for the Man Who Shut Me Up 14
Psychology Today: Narcissus and Echo 15
The Dear, The Dark 16
Ghazal: Moon 17
Selenotrope 18
Flawed. 19

III. ANAGRAMMES

[a mean gram] 23
[attract. else lie.] 25
[our omen, innit?] 27
[poet, AI-scared] 28
demimondaine 29

[f.u. wish] 30
[one mind. tea] 31
[o, brief de{r}angel] 33
[feign holy flame] 34
[ravage this] 35

IV. PLAGUE POEMS

Lemons 39
Mrs. Epidemiologist 40
Friable 41
de monstrorum 42
Whelm 43
Ghazal: Sea 44

V. THE FURIES

a hero[in]ic crown, with index 45

VI. MYSTICAL VISIONS OF SAINTS AND SINNERS

Inferno 65
Purgatorio 66
Paradiso 67
End Words 68
Penitential 69
Gravid 71
Mid-September 72
Velar 74

ACKNOWLEDGMENTS 77
NOTES 81

I.

GROUP THERAPY FOR THE FEMALE CHARACTERS OF *THE ODYSSEY*

Penelope

I tell them, though they never get it right:
I stood beside that pillar, my full height
(Athena-wrought Pilates)—it was me,
my strength and cunning were the husbandry
that kept our house erect. I used my looks
—I mean both: glances, veilèd, and my hook:
my beauty (if a little wrinkled now)—
but still they wanted me. I was their sow,
domestic; they, the rustic rutting boars
the very root of *hybrid,* it would seem,
the root also of *hubris.* Semen, seme:
the men are praised for coming back from wars.
I held our house together, son unharmed,
and I will be remembered for my charms.

Siren

I sing a song, dismembering, a charm
both dangerous and diligent. More harm
than good, my reputation—but my song:
a dark and smoky brew, Lapsang Souchong.
I softly croon and whisper [sex] a breath
of elemi that sounds and smells like death.
You've tied your stubborn captain to the mast.
You turn away, you warm the wax—Avast!
What if I said I only want your ear,
your full attention, turned toward me, erect.
If you could just oblige I wouldn't wreck
your ship, your self-esteem, your plans. *To hear*—
it's not the same—if you can't learn *to listen,*
your bird-pecked skeleton and skull will glisten.

Circe

You, peckish, skin-and-bones: I'll have you glisten-
ing, sweat and pheromones. Come closer: listen.
My island welcomes you, a second home,
by which I mean, you'll never be alone.
By witch—[you call me bitch?]—I see through you,
your pains, your muscles strained, your psyche bruised.
I offer wine and honey, sex and food.
You, men, you grab my girls, you're rough and rude
and you have no idea. I know what glisters
is all too often not a precious metal,
not silver, gold. I opt, then, not to settle.
I'll put you on the spit, and watch you blister,
your incense: fragrant meaty smoke. You swine,
you always knew you'd turn out to be mine.

Scylla

I'd always hoped you'd turn out to be mine,
you powerful, you handsome, you so fine—
whoever you were: politician, god:
to your high pinnacle I'm just a sod.
Whatever tale you tell, I'm now the beast,
the once-a-beauty, now the thing with teeth,
Picasso-monster, vagina dentata.
So what about you, with your armada
of lawyers, lovers tricked into collusion?
You treat me as the lesser of two evils.
You really want me to go all medieval
on your fine ass, like some foregone conclusion?
You mess with me, it's all gonna go south.
And mister, master, better watch my mouth.

Charybdis

The mist. The masticated. Watch my mouth:
    (I suck it in. I retch. I spit it out.)
They worry when they scuttle through my straits.
    (I worry terribly about my weight.)
I taste, I chew, I swallow, then I purge.
It's violent, it's swirly, it's my urge
    [*there's nothing tastes as good as being thin*]
and so I let you at me, sink and swim.
Oh, long ago, they said, *A pretty face*—
    [control, the water scrolls,
      the basin holds what they extol]
at least you have that, darling. Coup de grâce.
The goddess Beauty scratches at my soul.
I'll heave you, believe me, from pole to pole.

Nausikaa

I heaved him from the beach. I had to pull
him in, exhausted, thirsty, sun-mad, full
of sea-salt and nostalgia. When he woke
he said some words, a name, and then he choked
his tears back. I could see it was a game—
no—more a strategy, a way to claim
his presence with me. Then he took my hand
and looked into my eyes—I swear no man
has ever looked so deeply in me since.
He had no clothes. I gave him mine to wear.
I rubbed his skin with oil, I combed his hair.
He smelled of sun-baked juniper and incense.
We laughed and talked. He said he missed his home.
He wished for me I'd never be alone.

Eurykleia

Some days, I wished I'd had a different home.
It hurt my heart when every night she'd moan,
no way to know, she's crying or a dream
had taken her, the men downstairs who seemed
to overpower her despite her will.
I hardly slept at night at all until
I felt him out there, I knew he was near
(but I am old, invisible, my years,
they make me silent). So when he returned—
he nearly kicked my bucket, nearly choked
me right there on the spot. I sputtered, croaked—
I know you more than anyone. I've learned
the story isn't ever black or white.
I tell them, though they never get it right:

II.

SORORAL

E altro disse, ma non l'ho a mente;
    però che l'occhio m'avea tutto tratto
    ver' l'alta torre a la cima rovente,
dove in un punto furon dritte ratto
    tre furïe infernal di sangue tinte,
    che membra feminine avieno e atto,
e con idre verdissime eran cinte;
    serpentelli e ceraste avien per crine,
    onde le fiere tempie erano avvinte.

        . . . e gridavan sì alto,
ch'i' mi strinsi al poeta per sospetto.

    And more he said, but not in mind I have it;
    Because mine eye had altogether drawn me
Tow'rds the high tower with the red-flaming summit,
    Where in a moment saw I swift uprisen
    The three infernal Furies stained with blood,
    Who had the limbs of women and their mien,
    And with the greenest hydras were begirt;
    Small serpents and cerastes were their tresses,
Wherewith their horrid temples were entwined.

        . . . they cried so loud,
That I for dread pressed close unto the Poet.

—Dante, *Inferno*

Arachne

un triolet sbagliato
for a very mean professor

Don't fuck with the goddess
they all said, but I was naïve.
I was really good, y'know?—not being immodest—
but don't fuck with a goddess.

Perceived as hubris, an estro-test of wills, it's the oddest
thing: I simply loved—yes, lived—to weave.
I wanted her to see what I'd achieved.

I fucked with the goddess.
And tangled in this tiny web, I grieve.

Elegy for the Man Who Shut Me Up

    Sad. Everyone's sad
on the Social. You're dead. You
      tried to shut me up.

    Truth be told, it worked
for a while. I closed myself
      tight as a seashell

    as if aphasic;
I rocked for comfort, years lost.
      What was it scared you?

    Nice girls don't put out?
You're a healthy specimen,
      aren't you? Here, feel shame.

    Laid into us, drunk
maybe. Your distress, our mess-
      y, mollusky, muscl-

    ed feminine selves
that won't open for you, no
      matter how you prise.

    You tried to shut us
down. I'm here to tell you now,
      No such luck, buddy.

Psychology Today:
Narcissus and Echo

Narcissism is hot.
                                      What
Narcissists are so powerfully appealing
                                      is this feeling?
because you feel blessed when,
                                      Destined,
even if momentarily,
                                      unwarily
the bright beam of their self-
                                      bared. Melt-
love turns and shines on you.
                                      down to rue.
The narcissist's heart is closed,
                                      Bulldozed,
but he is often highly skilled
                                      sighing, thrilled.
at getting all he wants
                                      Goal of the hunt
through lying, passive-aggression,
                                      my flesh and
manipulation, and control,
                                      soul?
leaving his victim exhausted,
                                      Lost it.
feeling she has no choice.
                                      O, voice.

The Dear, The Dark

She tells me that she doesn't like the dark;
she's terrified that she'll dissolve in it.
I want to tell her, there's a certain art
to living in it. Ebony or jet,

black jade or onyx, these are precious things
without which one cannot behold the light
as it's meant to be seen: contradistinct:
the warmly luminous, the sweetly bright.

A perfect diamond on black velvet; stars
that shoot or sparkle in the evening sky;
the single candle in the funeral parlor;
the lighthouse beacon. She's about to cry

so now I'll tell her: it's a gift to know
the way the light emerges out of shadow.

Ghazal: Moon

Neil Armstrong bounced and pronounced on the moon.
My 7th birthday staring at the moon.

Wrack in runes, out of tune, "I nearly swooned."
What does it mean to be ruled by the moon?

Shot white wax in the blueblack sky,
smooth skin, cool music, full moon.

"Pull and swell and river to oblivion":
a barren woman contemplates the moon.

The Forum's disco-backlit: green, red, blue.
Through Colosseum arches, the scimitar moon.

Opalescent, moody, multiply tattooed,
selenotropic sisters praise the moon.

Old, Snow, Sap, Grass, Milk, Rose, Thunder Moon.
Green Corn, Fruit, Harvest, Frost, Long Night Moon.

In a poem composed in Greek, the sea
is silvered, slivered, fingers of the moon.

While haply She sits upon her throne,
dull lovers, soul-split, weep beneath the moon.

A mistress harsh and cold in reputation.
A lake of wavy onyx, mirrored moon.

Wolf, Snow, Worm, Pink, Flower, Strawberry Moon.
Buck, Corn, Harvest, Hunter's, Beaver, Cold Moon.

"It is not the moon, I tell you."
But it is, yes, it is, always, the moon.

Selenotrope

    Legend has it that
Li Po leaped into the moon's
    reflection, late night

    drunk, disordered on
wine and poems, the river
    dark and delicious.

    Scholars maintain it
was cirrhosis or poison,
    a toxic Taoist

    elixir brewed of
mercury and misplaced hopes
    for longevity.

    Longevity. Ha.
Who hasn't, lugubrious,
    brooded over it.

    Who wouldn't want to
embrace that satellite's sad
    light on a dark night

    of the soul, the space
between real and possible
    grown astronomical.

Flawed.

I never do exactly as I should.
I broke the vase, re-rearranging flowers
and "perfect is the enemy of good."

The painting teacher told us that it's good
to lay down light, then dark, in watercolors.
I never do exactly as I should.

The little girl who squished about in mud.
Parental expectations, sweet, then soured
when perfect was the synonym of good.

I left behind that lovely boy who would
have married me (*fair creature of an hour*):
I never do exactly as I should.

The coulda, woulda, shoulda: all wormwood
and hazardous to psyche: all devour,
as does the Perfect, enemy of good.

At dawn, that polyglottal poet stood,
his arms outstretched, atop Martello Tower.
*I never do exactly as I should
and perfect is the enemy of good.*

III.

ANAGRAMMES

[unfit lyres]

[silent fury]

[a mean gram]

so you already knew all these,
the list of complaints, black ink, white sheet,

your day completely gone to shit
and then it further hits

the proverbial fan, splatters,
stinks like rats' pelts

left out in brutal weather.
how to withstand the wear

and tear
of this low-rent, low-rate

existence, as if you haven't lived
till you've cut your deal with the devil?

I did it, gave myself o'er to the fire,
temptation, the life rife

with addictive proclivities,
    epic vitriols,

incalescent lust.
the judgment was pronounced: slut.

Gift means poison in German.
sweet little babe in a manger,

replaced on his day by a jolly fat Santa.
funny how they all wear red. Satan,

minacious, plunging from the skies,
give me your best embrace. kiss

the Daddy's girl: parental,
all and only is paternal.

[anagramme]

[attract. else lie.]

Hwæt. Yo. Aloha,
bad boy, you, a halo

of frizzy IOU curls,
demeanor all curious

and marsupial cute,
pure lamia cuts

straight outta Keats:
you've thrust your steampunk stake

into my heart.
My solitary, homey art.

Now what? Now: Detonated
is what, *tanto, tanto:* don weed

of widowdom, gutted;
hold in tow god (muted

for a change). Prescient,
the alcoholic's secret nip,

booze on flare on fire.
O, fine felon, fairer

than anyone ever, embrace
me, these amber eve rec-

konings, night's perfume
nascent, grief spent. Hum

alongside me, ever united,
even when the line's untied.

[a little. a secret.]

[our omen, innit?]

sitting here twiddling
fingers, wistful legend hid, writ

not in water but on a screen
so plain and mean no sane crone

would deign to touch
it, a dark so dark i'm induced to goth.

then! o joy, a popup! WINEBAR.
oh. wait. no, it's just a webinar:

"how to succeed on zoom!" [so much *merda*]
musing, fusing the old sweet dream

of connection. o, poor brain, your re-wired
synaptics, a path so hapless & weird

I long lovingly for a getaway.
but all we got's this cut-rate gateway

to a buncha boring left-brained tips
    [and no delicious sniff and swirl and spit]

—ring lamp; silkscarf-swathe; firm pout:
we're all so stunning from the waist up.

eff and blind this endless winding Safari
of roads untouched, each as just as fair.

                                             [monitor ennui]

[poet, AI-scared]

what does voice mean
anyhow? a nice move

into territories unknown?
weird kin, runes won

the hard way, in the interstices?
an ellipsis reticent

in a pause so pregnant
paper bloats and pens rot? nag

that muse, the rag and bone shop:
    ash, porn, bondage.

chanting, pour the libations;
bipolar out the sin.

sometimes, she's all about the silence.
rumor has it she lent ice

to athena: aunt, hymen, owl,
busy embodying the unwomanly.

busy being. hm. like *hymenoptera*
    [to self, note: harpy me]

that Order [n^{th} ages' shit]
in which, typically, the female has the sting.

                                     [arsed poetica]

demimondaine

he tried to flip the myth,
    fell in love with what she was,
opium den-
    izen, red silk shot
        through with slivers of silver:

ineluctable slo-mo to diss.
    do vipers hiss
before they strike?
    demonized, denied
        (she'd never lied)

she was something out of Nin,
    (o, the sin, the sin).
ever diva, ever avid:
    who dare demean her in her own
        demesne? (o, the shame).

her body, her temple,
    ever the fine mien
(dizzied, eddied)
    spreadeagled on the
        (she didn't mean to)
            kilim.

[f.u. wish]

To speke of wo that is in mariage

out the window, the whitecaps
look a lot like the epic swath

of her mood this afternoon, free-range
spitting catscratch anger.

no, let's be honest: it's rage,
salt and hollow shells thrown up with sea grit.

some days she resents the witch-lapse;
feels like 'twas he clip-

ped the wings, switched her to bitch, any rightful itch
twitched to high frailty. can't.

not a position tenable.
so she tells herself, let bane

go, clear out the vases to put
in new peonies. may poet thus stave

off her blues, find some wabi-sabi
in all of this, a bonsai-midwife bass-

line, a little kintsugi
to let the sunlit gilt kite

rise in the sky. nothing gold can stay,
as they say, and as the longings chant today.

[huswif]

[one mind. tea]

i'm losing my mind,
she says, her voice grown dim

and slow on the messenger
call. her, me, geneses:

she taught me to read,
how to adore

her careful letters on the chalkboard.
this is how you keep your mind broad.

now she's living with my sister: set
the scene (bonjour tristesse)

for greek drama
born of wildchild karma.

what's that word again, it starts with a D?
her memory a shard, it twists

and turns, turns traitor.
rain. rust. tort,

this brain-change is fuel
for nightmares out of fuseli.

at 3 a.m. she's afraid:
up surge the old dire sheafs,

hope and nostalgia,
the bleating of a slain goat.

she wakes, makes a cup of tea.
the drip, drip, drip of faucet

left on is not our fear: synapses
brittle as shaky aspens:

not just cranial fog,
we fear the conflagration.

[on dementia]

[o, brief de{r}angel]

today the wind blew in, boreal
and truculent. no comfort, not in fine labor

nor in love. someone very dear
has died: poet, friend, wildely read

—he of silver beard
prodigious, he who bared

psyche, soul. confessional,
he spilled the stygian noises, flacon

of the anima, a prised
precision of despair—

cigar smoke wafts on air
bereft. he's left us here.

in his death I relive
all those my dearests; revile

the damned, dark dearth.
who is it snips the thread?

the one i'm named after?
myrrh, dark berry, bitter fate?

[an elegie for dr b]

[feign holy flame]

intaglioed in my heart, broad-
shouldered Quasimacho, bard

of bastardry, of badassery.
ever at the verge of his dear abyss,

how he delighted in dreadness:
metaphysical dark, the sad, red, *sen-*

za sensibility. fine wine and siren
song. who knows who holds the reins

in a life, anyway? cloak blown about
as if on moors; law, taboo unblock-

ed. this is no fiction, no hyperbole:
falling in slo-mo, noble hyperion,

always the ice-eyed wolf-
dog by his side. he left behind wife, cold eye

cast. left behind children too,
no glance back, no salt pillar. and no hit colder:

the daughter who knows he must go, rue leapt
clean o'er. memory the sweet rogue petal.

[gone half my life]

[ravage this]

what to leave at his [anathema] grave,
Mexican-sugar Coke, bitter agave?

all the shoulds, woulds, coulds?
gray, the negative-capable clouds

   [subjunctive funk of weather]
slide by, a grief-lade wreath

on black granite. sharply carved
the name, water-writ, craved

fame. wisdom wit or wist, Mentor,
master of subtle torments,

to him i raise this chalice, rim
dipped [sugar, salt, citrus]. chimerical

the blessèd boozy bluesy moods
and all nine muses bloody

in his wake. yet: éminence grise, beloved
sometimes, solely to verse obliged.

left so lonely, i can only listen,
sitting cross-legged, silent

                                          [at his grave]

IV.

PLAGUE POEMS

"Unde haec, o Palinure, tibi tam dira cupido?
Tu Stygias inhumatus aquas amnemque severum
Eumenidum aspicies, ripamve iniussus adibis?"

"What hopes delude thee, miserable man?
Think'st thou, thus unintomb'd, to cross the floods,
To view the Furies and infernal gods,
And visit, without leave, the dark abodes?"

—Virgil, *Aeneid*

Lemons

Citrine rings of sun
   steep in hot water,
the blue-and-white china cup
   a gift from a friend. Distant.
We are all distanced.
No one is immune.

Mrs. Epidemiologist

Where we
    don't kiss,
don't mix spit;
only rarely now in anger
   do I hiss
(cat claws, complaints useless):
our little house.
    Sun shines outside, bliss.

And outside you persist.
Stay away from us
    (please)
o, little virus.

Friable

I ask my mother
    to tell me
what she remembers
    of my father
as she nursed him in his final days.
Gaunt, nearly gone, his bones
    extruded; friable
the skin. She was tender
    arranging the catheter
that poured the poison in.

    She knelt before him,
long years divorced,
    years longing. One day,
she says, he reached out
    to touch her temple.
"So pretty. Did you dye it?"
    She laughed.
"No, Mike, I'm just
    going gray."

de monstrorum

Then a friend tells me
that during isolation
her unconscious has been
bubbling up, La Brea tar pits,
scenes re-remembered,
secrets she didn't tell me
because too dark and awful,
rank smell of sugar and sex.

Exes are texting,
according to *The New York
Times*. Sometimes I think of this
one or that. *Where is he now?*
I wonder, distant.
But no texts. Last night I dreamed
that a girl with pink dreadlocks
and a medusa

tattoo on her skull
came up to me and hugged me.
And I averted my face.
It's gone viral, I shouted
in the dream. What did I mean?
Medusa was the only
mortal gorgon. Don't even
try to look her in the eyes.

Whelm

Note from a friend:
"So sorry I haven't written: I'm just
overwhelmed.
Overused, undermeant—you
know, I hate to say that word." I

know. But I can't help wonder,
overwhelm? I
know the
over but the *whelm*? *Middle English:* to turn

over, capsize, turn upside down.
No surprise. Perhaps from
Old English: arched, concave. *Icelandic:*
overturn. *Ancient Greek:*
κόλπος, bosom, hollow, gulf. And

though I have a house, a
home, and know how fortunate I am,
oh, when I see that word,
overwhelm, sea-tossed,
lonely, I think of that
prodigious wave. Tsunami. And
oh, the terrible sigh.
Hokusai.

Ghazal: Sea

(with a final couplet by E. E. Cummings)

As Karen Blixen said, the cure's the sea
—or sweat, or tears—but I prefer the sea.

In fact, it's homeopathy. Why cry
with eyes baptized (if reddened) by the sea?

The metaphors of fabric come to mind:
cool silk or aqua velvet, summer sea

> (or better, come to *body:* intimate,
>   enveloped skin on skin, the lover sea).

The bone-ache deep, the pains gone unexplained:
for now just dive, ameliorator sea.

The "mermaid's tears," smoothed glass or plastic: lovely
but hazardous to creatures of the sea.

This evening's rough: Poseidon snaps my straps.
Pathetic fallacy, bipolar sea.

And in their one-piece suits, the ladies age
and silver, laugh and rage: September sea.

For whatever we lose(like a you or a me)
it's always ourselves we find in the sea

V.

THE FURIES

(a hero[in]ic crown,
with index)

ΧΟΡΟΣ
(μυγμὸς διπλοῦς ὀξύς.)

λαβὲ λαβὲ λαβὲ λαβέ, φράζου.

CHORUS MEMBER
(grumbling: doubly loud, keener)

Get him! Get him! Get him! Get him! *Focus*!

—Aeschylus, *Eumenides*

The women in the courtyard play with clay,
the squishy earth worked smooth and glistening.
They're sculpting hybrids: gorgons, sirens, sphinx.
One fettles fine a mermaid's arms and tail.
Her friend says, *Hey, those boobs, they're way
too big. She'd sink.* I say, *No, she would float*
[which brings to mind an awful sexist joke
about Mae West, which I refuse to say].

Another asks, *Why is it always us
deformed, made monster, harpy, mythic bitch?
They're satyrs, centaurs, brandishing huge dicks.*
 —Can you remind me what a harpy is?
*A shrieking bird, a woman's ugly visage.
She'll take your wedding cake and shit on it.*

Persephone's and Hades's wedding cake
must have been topped with pomegranate seeds
and iced with Lethe-colored buttercream.
Imagine that you have to consummate
this union born of taking what he takes,
oblivious to struggles and your screams,
oblivious to other plans and dreams.
Imagine that in every U.S. state
the law, until the 1970s
(*If You Can't Rape Your Wife, Who[m] Can You Rape?*)
allowed a man to take his wife, to seize
and bruise and batter her, if he should please.
Imagine how the verb *to ravish* might
have morphed from *rape* to *filling with delight.*

Rapunzel, rampion, affright.
The woebegone of barrenness.
But did she wish to reproduce?
Her slavish cravings in the night
might show another wish, despite.
The witch's realm, the garden rich,
emmenagogic herbs and such
could cause the loss by firelight.

    the ivory tower prison
    where access is forbidden
    unless the code is broken.

a pussy-grabbing president
the overturn of precedent
a vessel that is only meant

A Vestal virgin in her element.
No images allowed, she tends the flame
of hearth (or heart or art), each day the same.
She serves, unswerving, Goddess immanent,
the sacrosanctifying imminent.
The sympathetic Muse observes her, pained.
She sits or kneels or walks, complexion drained,
perhaps a little tired of being patient.

Sometimes she dreams of Vesta, asteroid
the third in size and brightest of the night.
She knows the circumscription of her orbit,
orbitofrontal cortex just annoyed.
Perhaps she'll rapture out one final fight
in time to bust a rupture in her habit.

What was the woman doing with the tablet
in her lap? Why did the archaeologists
have to ask? Well, obvious: the voicelessness
a given. Did she not write hymns and sonnets
to sun and moon and blood and distant planets?
Of course you've heard the joke: Anonymous
was woman, woman-born, to take the piss;
her silly work: the critics piss upon it.

My friend sent me an essay. "Stamina"
(*from Latin, plural,* stamen, *in the sense
of threads spun by the Fates*). Enheduana
persisted: poet, priestess, "ornament
of heaven." *My lord, that which here has been
created no one has created before.*

No one's created quite like this before.
She sits beside the gauzy window, lone,
scrapes at her palette, scrapes down to the bone,
examining her true self in the mirror.
Her eyes are large and clear, confront the viewer.
If these are windows to her soul, she owns
the very elements around her, stone
and fire, earth and air, and brilliant color.

Who was she then? *The Origin of Painting*?
"You have to look a model in the face
to apprehend the soul, you have to delve
down deep for truth, to tell that tale on canvas.
You have to look your model in the face,
no fakes, no kindness; truth a kind of grace."

Self-Portrait as the Second of Three Graces
Self-Portrait as a Disembreasted Saint
Self-Portrait as the Allegory of Painting
Self-Portrait as Picasso's Nightmare Faces

Self-Portrait as the Blue of Autumn Skies
Self-Portrait as a Poet at Her Desk
    Whose Ghosts Surround Her, Anything But Blessed
Self-Portrait as a Woman with No Eyes

Self-Portrait as the Xanthophyllic Leaves
Self-Portrait as Lachesis, Clad in Black
Self-Portrait as the Adjunct Asst. Professor
    a Month Away from Sleeping in Her Car
Self-Portrait as Bloodshot Insomniac
Self-Portrait as the One Who Only Grieves

Another poet bites the dust. They grieve
most openly and throatfully: "He blurbed
my second book." "In faith he never swerved . . ."
I have a different story. Please believe
I mean no disrespect, but he, one evening
was asked to name some *women poets* whom
he loved, admired. A silence. Then a hem,
a haw; his helpful friend tugged at his sleeve—

> [while in this auditorium there sat
> a dozen noted *women poets,* eyes
> downcast in what? anger? reflected shame?]

"Well, Sappho. Dickinson of course—and what's
her name, I chose her book once for a prize—
yes, Jane, Jane, can't remember her last name."

And yes, it's plain, we must reclaim the names
they hurtle at us. Vixen, harridan,
virago, harpy, nag, hag, termagant,
she-devil, fishwife, hellcat, *la belle dame
sans merci* (though I do wonder, where's the shame
in being merciless at times). Gorgon,
old bag, old bat, old trout, old cow, dragon.
A bitch so mythic there's no one to blame

but maybe you. I learned another choice
vocabulary word the other day:
it's *fawning,* a response to complex trauma.
We smile, we shrink, we charm, avoiding drama.
Of course, my dear, it's never what you say
but I cannot unhear your tone of voice.

"Sometimes, my dear, it seems my very voice
annoys you. What to do? Change timbre? Pitch?
Intensity? Stuck in your craw? My sitch?
If hearing's given, listening's a choice
that I don't think you choose. I take up space
—or try to, anyway, discussion nixed
when my poor mouth I open. What's the fix
that you'd propose? I'm all ears, you're all voice.

"Elective mute myself? Electrocute
myself? Go glottal, velar, labio-
dental? Go mental? Head toward the river
with stones in pockets? Oh, I don't think so.
Whatever angle, straight, obtuse, acute,
I'm out to take it back, Indian giver."

It's hard to write a poem with a fever
despite the precedents of history:
of Plath, her out-of-body 103,
or deathbed Keats, his final days a river
of sweat and blood, hope whittled to a sliver
> *O! I can feel the cold earth upon me*
> *—the daisies growing over me—*
How blest he was in Severn, who outlived him.

Our sweet friend died, the early weeks of covid.
He'd just retired, wanted to be a poet
and play guitar full-time. What have we learned?
No masks, no vaxx, logic and science turned
to enemy. Their signs scream **It's my body
it's my choice.** Ah, blissful blessèd irony.

I was not interested in irony;
I tried to emphasize the primacy
of the idea in making art. *The irony
was work itself became, probably,
my poetry's best subject.* At times like these,
the thing we need is scorching irony,
not argument. *A deeper and less friendly
understanding comes out of irony.*

In a world where irony reigns,
in which you separate, protect and laugh
at anything honest or with an emotional
charge—I bet for catharsis—And catharsis,
when it's touched the emotional vein,
can open doors of even those who've closed.

Head bangs against the door. Never enough
to rise above the risible
to view beyond the visible
to clear the channel, staticky, to slough
the Slough of Despond off. To learn to tough
it out, the mire of miserable
the insult of invisible,
Houdini out the existential 'cuffs.

I know, Bitch, right, where is your gratitude?
How far you think you'll get with this attitude?
You think I'm gonna go there with some platitude,
and you'd be right. *The irony of life*
is hardly anyone gets out alive.
And bees are not returning to their hive.

I found a dead bee on my bedroom floor
the other day. A long way from the hive,
a clear-cut apian case of failure to thrive.
Poor thing, so glad I didn't step on her
—not least, a miracle to remember
that even when they're dead they keep the sting,
the venom stays there, still a nasty thing.
I made a careful tissue coffin for her

and carried her outside. The wind picked up,
the clouds fast-forwarded from white to gray.
My neighbor called across the fence: Hey, join us.
We're dancing to ward off the hurricane.
It's never going to work, but what the fuck,
us women in the garden, feet of clay.

Index

A Vestal virgin in her element:
And yes, it's plain, we must reclaim the names.
Another poet bites the dust, they grieve,
Head bangs against the door. Never enough.
I found a dead bee on my bedroom floor.
I was not interested in irony.
It's hard to write a poem with a fever;
No one's created quite like this before:
Persephone's and Hades's wedding cake,
Rapunzel, rampion, affright.
Self-Portrait as the Second of Three Graces:
Sometimes, my dear, it seems my very voice.
The women in the courtyard play with clay;
What was the woman doing with the tablet?

VI.

MYSTICAL VISIONS OF SAINTS AND SINNERS

Tunc primum lacrimis victarum carmine fama est
Eumenidum maduisse genas.

> Then, for the first time ever,
> the Furies' cheeks were wet with tears,
> conquered by the poem's power.
>
> —Ovid, *Metamorphoses*

Inferno

A night walk in a dark wood, heartwood hard and hearkened. The crackle and smoke of a fire, just beyond the next hill. Bawls and caterwauls of distant beasts: leopard, lion, wolf. The rank skank of sex and ego, pheromones and fear. You want what you want. Slo-mo slog through slough through sloth; a sudden brush of breeze clicks through the black leaves. A wickedly strabismal glint of topaz. You have never felt so lost in all your life, so you take the hand offered. Where you will go is even deeper, darker: the sulphurous scent of descent.

                top notes: smoke. rafflesia. fleurs du mal.
                middle notes: asphodel. oud. camphor.
                base notes: hyraceum. tar. phenol.

Purgatorio

The slippery slope, the *limen,* light or dark. Which pulls you more? The sunset shadows dance, seductive, red, white, black. Pride, prick and prickle, price or praise. What did you covet, what then did you crave? Just pull away, the way you know you should. O guilt of pleasure, pleasure guilt, the gate. The sweaty climb, sublime, the primerose hill. Presume. Preclude. *Prie-dieu.* Your epic dreams (wrong epic), gates of ivory and of horn. You postulant, you penitent, you fragile flagellant, you black-strap whip. The deep rose speaks so sweetly yet too well you know its thorns.

> **top notes:** damascena. pomegranate. vetiver.
> **middle notes:** indole. leather. frankincense.
> **base notes:** opoponax. sandalwood. myrrh.

Paradiso

The liquid air is soft and clean; you sip it more than breathe. As if enveloped in white velvet, calm, she takes your hand in hers and guides you on. Her eyes are cobalt, piercing as the noonday sky. You have the sudden sense of being seen: no vales, no veils, no lies. The Sunday bells begin to chime, the Ave's rhyme. The lilting, lulling music: all is perfectly in time. A rose explosion, sunlit notes of innocence and clarity. The light so bridal white it's almost blue; the sweet so sweet it's almost bitter, distant as the stars.

top notes: white rose. aldehydes. jasmine.
middle notes: Chamaelirium luteum. acqua santa. virgin's bower.
base notes: white amber. castoreum. white pine.

End Words

                              Magdalene
                 apse
                      synapse
                              religion

               connection
                         perhaps
                    lapse
                        unction

                                                      hair
                                                      sin
                                                    alone

                                                        air
                                                      kin
                                                   stone

Penitential

    (Titian, Artemisia, Caravaggio, Ambrosius Benson)

She's nude but for the bestial pelt of hair
that cataracts, thick gold and red;
cascades around her breasts, leaving them bare.
The perfect amphiboly of her gaze
of ecstasy and pain in equal parts.
One hand protects her heart.

Theatrically she clutches at her heart.
Her gown is golden luscious, but her hair
is frazzled, as if rent, as if this part
is not quite done; relinquishing the red,
the madder, ruddled soul of sin. That gaze
(within, without) leaves her completely bare.

And though she's richly clothed she wears a bare
expression of despair. The maudlin heart.
Her head's inclined; her earthward-facing gaze
inscrutable; the uncombed strands of hair.
A single tear; her face is splotched with red.
Perfume; a strand of pearls that's come apart.

The graceful fingers, held apart
to prise the jar of unguent. Bare
and clear the myrrh and frankincense, a red
and black olfaction. Necklace at her heart;
so much in shadow: velvet bodice, hair.
Is that a smile? or dark and downcast gaze?

(And you: don't frame yourself within that gaze
        nor come apart
      and never rend your hair
            nor bare

your barren heart.
Utter red,

        blood red
    the bloodshot gaze,
        ever more weary the heart
    you've learned to hold apart,
you've learned to bear.

    Never let down your hair.)

Gravid

    (Piero della Francesca)

If pregnant women don't have to pay
  the entrance fee, then what about me?
The Madonna del Parto gazes
  (eyes inscrutable, fingers slitting
apertures in the celestial blue)
  straight to my center of gravity.
Her strange angels seem one wingèd, in-
  complete, grasping the heavy curtains,
opening, closing them, who's to say?

  Long ago, a gypsy predicted
for me two daughters, one dark, one fair.
  Grief and guilt come in colors, dull red,
queasy green. I said no to nature,
  then nature turned and said no to me.
Frescoes pale with the passage of years,
  or they crack and chip during earthquakes;
shadings and lines grow ever less clear.
  But this sinopia never fades.

Mid-September

That lone turtledove
    [objective correlative?]
coos, moodily coos—
        Don't they always come in twos?
        How does she know to perch here

on my rafter, me
    alone with my sunset glass
of wine, perfect shade
    to complement the rosé
    of the clouds, the darkening

sky. She peers at me,
    eyes seemingly wise, myrtle
or juniper fruit.
    Grateful for her company,
    I toss olive bits her way.

The widow next door
    waits every night for her son
to get home. Haloed
    by the light of her TV,
    she watches the broadcast news.

I didn't know her
    back then, that night her husband
didn't make it home.
    Electrical accident.
    Life's like that, she always says.

Yes, I think. And so
    is death. Philosophical,
my friend asks, *Isn't
    it all temporary, all?*
    Indeed. I know the sea needs

not me to say how
 beautiful it is, deep blue
glazed with silver haze,
 the sudden break to turquoise.
 White cliffs across the channel,

whitecaps and wind-wails.
 Today not a single sail-
boat. The days grow short,
 fade to liminal shades, pink,
 orange, gray. [Is that redundant?

Fade, liminal, shade?]
 This summer I didn't see
a single falling
star.

Velar

She said that faith is her anchor
but I heard anger.

Fragile, fraught faith,
bells and beeswax candles a base-

less base, frankincense
and myrrh, common sense

thrown
out the stained-glass window.

Those characters
we studied in the Minster

windows, transluced
as through a membrane, luteous.

A medieval monk with spectacles
round like vintage Elton's.

Who knew that kind of vision was possible
back then? Her son a suicide, impassable

the life, ever unable
to translate love from the cradle

to where he was. Once
I touched a page of vellum

made of fetal calfskin. Buttery, as they say
in the trade.

Disruptive to the systems, anger
or anchor.

Both velar. One voiced,
one voiceless.

ACKNOWLEDGMENTS

Deepest gratitude to the editors of the following publications in which the poems noted below first appeared (sometimes in slightly different versions):

Action, Spectacle: three from "The Furies" crown ("No one's created quite like this before," "Self-Portrait as the Second of Three Graces," and "What was the woman doing with the tablet"); *Axon: Creative Explorations:* "[a mean gram]," "[o, brief de{r}angel]," "[one mind. tea]"; *Ergon: Greek/American & Diaspora Arts and Letters:* "Group Therapy for the Female Characters of *The Odyssey*" ("Charybdis," "Circe," "Eurykleia," "Nausikaa," "Penelope," "Scylla," and "Siren"); *Five Points:* three from "The Furies" crown ("Head bangs against the door. Never enough," "I found a dead bee on my bedroom floor," and "I was not interested in irony"); *Hampden-Sydney Poetry Review:* "Arachne" and "The Dear, The Dark"; *Hopkins Review:* "Velar"; *Live Encounters: Poetry & Writing:* "[attract. else lie]," "[our omen, innit?]," and four from "The Furies" crown ("And yes, it's plain, we must reclaim the names," "Another poet bites the dust. They grieve," "It's hard to write a poem with a fever," and "'Sometimes, my dear, it seems my very voice"); *Smartish Pace:* "[feign holy flame]."

"Gravid" first appeared in *Feathers from the Angel's Wing: Poems Inspired by the Paintings of Piero della Francesca* (Persea Books, 2016).

"Psychology Today: Narcissus and Echo" first appeared in *Metamorphic: 21st Century Poets Respond to Ovid* (Recent Work Press, 2017).

"Ghazal: Moon" and "Selenotrope" first appeared in *Giant Steps: Fifty Poets Reflect on the Fiftieth Anniversary of the Apollo 11 Moon Landing and Beyond* (Recent Work Press, 2019).

"*de monstrorum,*" "Friable," "Lemons," "Mrs. Epidemiologist," and "Whelm" were included in WRITE Where We Are NOW, a project initiated during lockdown by Carol Ann Duffy and the Manchester Writing School at Manchester Metropolitan University.

"Inferno," "Paradiso," and "Purgatorio" first appeared in *Divining Dante* (Recent Work Press, 2021).

"Arachne," "The Dear, The Dark," "*de monstrorum,*" "Friable," "Ghazal: Moon," "Gravid," "Group Therapy for the Female Characters of *The Odyssey*" ("Charybdis," "Circe," "Eurykleia," "Nausikaa," "Penelope," "Scylla," and "Siren"), "Inferno," "Lemons," "Mrs. Epidemiologist," "Paradiso," "Purgatorio," and "Selenotrope" appeared (in English and Italian) in *Amore e morte: Poesie nuove e scelte* (Edizioni Tlon, 2022).

"[feign holy flame]" was a finalist for *Smartish Pace*'s Erskine J. Poetry Prize, 2024.

"Penitential" first appeared in *Dancing About Architecture and Other Ekphrastic Maneuvers* (MadHat Press, 2024).

"Velar" was also reprinted in *Best Spiritual Literature 2024* (Orison Books, 2024).

"Ghazal: Sea" was featured on the Academy of American Poets' "Poem-a-Day" on March 5, 2025.

Thanks to the St. Stephen's School in Rome for a sabbatical year that allowed me to finish writing this book. During that time, I was a Columbus School for Girls (CSG) Foundation Fellow at the Virginia Center for the Creative Arts (VCCA); particular thanks to Kevin O'Halloran, Sheila Gulley Pleasants, and the entire VCCA team for a delightful and productive stay, and for having taken such good care of me. Deepest gratitude to the Academy of American Poets for the honor of the Raiziss/de Palchi Translation Fellowship. During my Raiziss/de Palchi–affiliated residency at the American Academy in Rome (AAR), I learned that this book would be published; many thanks to the AAR for the time and space to work, not only on my stated project of translating Giorgiomaria Cornelio's poetry but on finalizing this manuscript as well. I am grateful to the Institute for Creative Writing and Literary Translation at John Cabot University for community, fellowship, and fun.

My heartfelt appreciation to James W. Long and the Louisiana State University Press team who helped me to bring this book into the world: Ashley Gilly, freelancer Susan Murray, Sunny Rosen, James Wilson, and Michelle Neustrom.

Tante tante grazie a:
Kim Addonizio, Derrick Austin, Judith Baumel, Gary & Jo Blankenburg, Catherine Carter, Chris Childers, Giorgiomaria Cornelio, Carol Ann Duffy, Dave Johnson, Jahan Khajavi, Ricardo Maldonado, Jeannie Marshall, James Davis May, Eric Mayer, Sandra Morelli, Elizabeth Mosier, Nikay Paredes, Chelsea Rathburn, Rebecca Raynor, Michael & Ilene Salcman, Jennifer Scappettone, Nicole Sealey, Alexis Sears, Graziella Sidoli, Dean Smith, Adrienne Su, John Taylor, David Yezzi.

As ever and always, deepest appreciation to my beloveds on both sides of the Atlantic: all of clan Egan, tutta la famiglia Abeni. And, finally and not least, to Damiano Abeni, my partner in translation as well as in life: *chapeau*.

NOTES

"Ghazal: Moon": The line "It is not the moon, I tell you" is from "Mock Orange," by Louise Glück.

EPIGRAPHS

To the book: *The Hymns of Orpheus,* Orphic Hymn no. 70. Translation by Thomas Taylor.

To Part II: *Dante's Inferno,* Canto IX. Translation by Henry Wadsworth Longfellow.

To Part IV: Virgil, *Aeneid,* Book 6. Translation by John Dryden.

To Part V: Aeschylus, *The Oresteia: The Eumenides.* Translation by Moira Egan.

To Part VI: Ovid, *Metamorphoses,* Book X. Translation by Moira Egan.

"THE FURIES" SONNET CROWN

Sonnet 2: The italicized question is drawn from the article "'But If You Can't Rape Your Wife, Who[m] Can You Rape?': The Marital Rape Exemption Re-Examined," *Family Law Quarterly* 15, no. 1 (Spring 1981): 1–29.

Sonnet 5: A few lines were inspired by Rossilynne Skena Culgan's article on Enheduana: "The World's First Writer Was a Woman and This New Exhibit at The Morgan Celebrates Her" (TimeOut.com, October 13, 2022).

Sonnet 6: The final lines are a statement on portrait painting by the artist Suzanne Valadon (1865–1938). Translation by Moira Egan.

Sonnet 10: The final line is inspired by the Method Man song "I Get My Thang in Action."

Sonnet 12: This cento/sonnet is composed of quotations by Sol LeWitt, Philip Levine, Frederick Douglass, Agnes Repplier, and Alejandro González Iñárritu, edited somewhat to somewhat fit the meter.

Sonnet 13: The italicized quote is attributed to Robert A. Heinlein.

www.ingramcontent.com/pod-product-compliance
Lightning Source LLC
Chambersburg PA
CBHW030122170426
43198CB00009B/710